SKELETAL SONGS

Decomposed

by

Stefan Duncan

I have a bone
to pick with you

Table of Contents

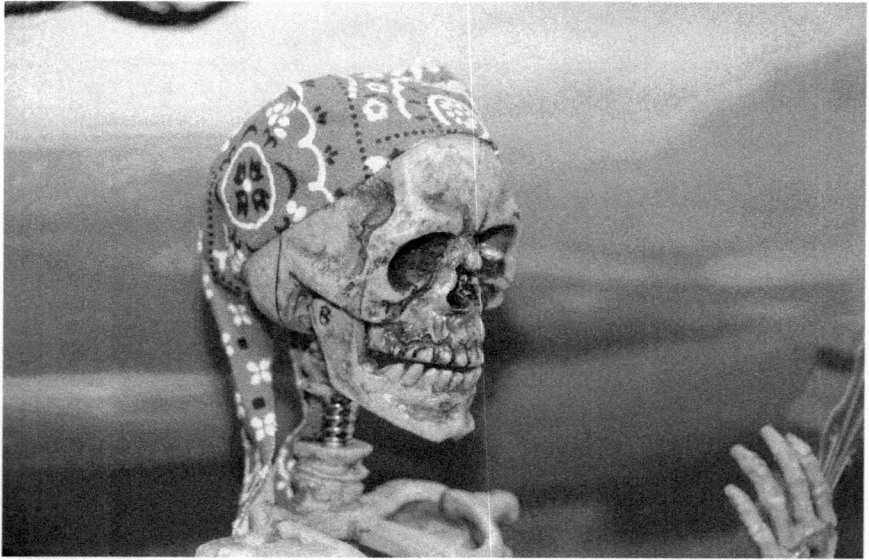

SKELETAL SONGS

Through the earth, we can hear the keys
Of the groundskeeper
As he locks the fence.

We crawl along the myriad
Of tunnels to the edge
Of the graveyard
And dig holes wide enough
For our skulls to push
Through the freshly mowed grass.

There is no song sweeter
Than a wolfish wind
Blowing through our mandibles.

Though our vocal chords have long since withered,
By the clatter of our teeth,
We sing love songs
To our women skeletals,
And give them flowers
From the new graves.

When it comes to love,
We make no bones about it.

TALE OF WACCAMAW LAKE

Belinda! Once and nevermore
I share our anniversary alone.
My heart aggrieved in destitute,
Beloved wife forever gone.

Agonizing it is to reminisce
The night adrift our wedding craft.
Still hearing our declarations of love
One summer night five years passed.

Pledging eternities with pounding hearts
Our echoes of passion abound,
Wedding night on Waccamaw
Beneath a sky filled with clouds.

In fear of water the way you were,
You ventured upon this craft
To spend our honeymoon as one
To be remembered with cherished laughs.

Oh horror! I woke to find her gone
Amid the Waccamaw Lake.
My beloved, she fell overboard
And ne'er did I awake.

Did she die in slumbered sleep?
That I'll never know
Except in sleep in nightmare's world
Where all is vividly told.

In terror she cried out my name,
Her hands missing the boat by an inch.
And lying there, in sleep so sound,
My body not moving, not even a flinch.

A thousand times my nightmares,
They jerk me from my bed.

2

My hand grasping out for hers,
To me she's never dead.

If only I could find her now,
Beneath the Waccamaw Lake.
I'd give to her my last of breath
And pray that she'll awake.

BRIDE OF FROGENSTEIN

Creatures leap into the water.
A silence falls around the pond,
Not even a cricket is heard.
The weeds part.
A large webbed foot appears,
Then another.
"It's Frogenstein!"
Ten inches tall,
Green from head to toe,
He lurches forward,
Stiffly walking
Toward the water's edge.
The monster descends.
Rigor mortis prevents him
From swimming.
He trudges along the bottom
With his throat-plugs sparking.

Where has my bride gone? He wonders.
He had worked so hard to find a dead
Frog to make her his wife.

For months, hiding in the weeds,
Catching fireflies with his tongue.
He strung them together, making a bed
And now lays a dead girl-frog on them.
With his most frightening *"RIP IT!"*
The fireflies flash
And sparks
Frogenstein's wife
Into life.
She opens her eyes and sees his face.
She screams and leaps into the water.
Poor Frogenstein cries.

Why does she hide? He wonders
With great despair,
And wipes a formaldehyde tear

4

With his tongue
And wishes wives could be mail ordered.

He spreads sticky saliva
Over a lily pad
And sprinkles living fireflies
To make a bed.
The operating table is prepared.

Soon it will be raining.
Frogenstein lurches to the roadside
Waiting for another dead bride
With enough guts to marry him.

HOMECOMING OF THE DEAD

The last station wagon
Leaves a trail of dust
Along the road to the church.
Pieces of tin foil
And paper plates tumble
Across the grass.

Behind the church,
In the graveyard,
The dead rise.
They help each other
Climb out of the graves
And enter the church.
One by one, they bathe
In the baptism, their
Bones shining like ivory.
Then, they stand under
The canopy in front of the church.

Those that had been members
Of the choir, dress in robes.
The director forms them into
A group by the picnic tables.
He stands on one leg,
For he takes a femur bone and uses
It to direct the choir to
Click with their teeth,
"Holy, Holy, Holy…." They sing.

The husbands pluck roses
Beside the steps. They
Pin them on their wives.
Prayer is clattered
By the preacher's still
Intact partials.

With a loud clacking *"Amen!"*
The skeletals sit before

Their invisible plates
And eat the hearty memories
Of the reunions gone past.

Laughter, fellowship,
The yearly reunion
A grand success.
The new comers are
Given special recognition.
They hug each other
Carefully not to
Entangle their ribs.

They say goodbye till next year
And return to their graves.
The preacher is the last
To descend, making sure
Each of his brothers
And sisters are properly bedded.

Monday morning.
Caretaker scratches his head.
Who redid the grave mounds?
When he cleans the picnic tables
He finds several teeth and toe joints.
He doesn't think of quitting until
He had noticed someone had
Plucked all the roses in the front of the church
And left a bony footprint in the dirt.

TO MY DAD, HOWARD WARD

I remember The Observer on Hay Street
With you up to your eyes in ink.
How you made five-pound weights from lead
And coached me into a great center fielder
By catching your golf balls with a brand new baseball glove
From your nine-iron swings.

When I begged you to throw me your fastest pitch
And caught it in the mitt of my gut.
When I missed a ball game from the cut on my leg
From hopping over a neighbor's fence
You took me to my first James Bond movie
And pointed out when 007 injured his leg
I was suddenly proud to bare the scar.
I watched your ascent from printer to sports editor.

And ever since, hardly anything's changed,
Except for new golf clubs and retiring from the paper.
Instead of coaching my sports, you edit my writing.
We saw "Die Hard," and we ate at our old restaurant prior to writing this.
Funny how I have a lift on the shoe of my right foot
And my Uncle Floyd, your brother, has one also from a car accident.
You're still golfing but with a little hobble now. I'm still hobbling.
We're both still writing. You with your sports … me with swords
For a while and now painting.
I produce the drama. You produce the scores.
Before the accident, I had eight books piled high
For you to edit.
Maybe one day, I wrote on this poem two decades ago, we'll score with a
scare.
2013 our first book was published.
And now this poem at last completed 23 years later.
Wow, just remembered
I can't remember
How old I was…but did a little drawing of a gator
For your story of a man's golfing experience while in a hazard
Twenty-three years later, we're still doing the stuff
Our second book, Raven's Light is about to come out

I emailed to tell you and knowing I'll be seeing you later.
And I also remember, I was 14 I and I had just learned the art of deception
by my cousin pretending I was 16 rather than 14 when she took me to a
party with her older friends.
Later you and I went to a restaurant and we promised never to lie to one
another.
It was a great heart-to-heart and I felt a great bond with you that day.
It reminded me when I was younger and I was due a spanking for
something.
Mom said wait until your father gets home.
You took me in the bathroom and closed the door.
You told me to cry out when you hit the tub with your belt.
Splashed water in my eyes to look like I was crying.
It sounded like I was dying.
Mom berated you for being so harsh.
And we smiled secretly to one another the rest of the night.

Remember the time we drove Uncle Wallace's station wagon
We couldn't go over 35
And a big rumbling truck passed
Leaving us with awful smell as it went by
We both looked at one another in disgust and laughed
With sprinkles of brown on the windshield dried
Then I saw your face covered in chicken poo
I laughed so hard I cried.

DON'T BE PARTIAL

(Poem To My Grandmother)

Grandma is a vampire.
So we pulled her teeth
While she slept.

Today a package
Came from U.P.S.
She got partial dentures –
Two ivory fangs.
She used super glue.
This time we'll have
To remove her gums.

A HOWL, A HOWL HOWL, A HOWL A HOWL

(Sing to tune of Bad To The Bone)

Werewolves in the city
Sniffing dirty streets
Looking for a person
Who's got the sweetest meat?
I can hear them howling
A howl a howl a howl a howl a howl

Born with the wolf blood,
They were born to be bad,
Wearing red laced Reeboks
Gettin' into the fad.

Can you feel their heartbeats
Before they chow for blood?
Are you the big bad wolf
Disguised as Robin Hood?

Do you salute the moonshine
Colored red, white, and black?
Do you wear a wolf coat
In your red Cadillac?

Here comes the moon now
A howl a howl a howl a howl a howl

Hollow- eyed and scabbed legs
Ravening wolf at night
Howling in the graveyards
Fangs itching for a bite

There's no need to worry
About the rising sun.
You're just a teenager
With teeth instead of guns.

A howl a howl a howl
A howl a howl

Who needs a werewolf
With terrorists all around
Cause anything that's worthy
Gonna get knocked down

THE WEREWOLF WALTZ

I dreamed my love
Transformed into a wolf.
I felt the prickling
Of hair, heard the sheath
Of claws growing from fingertips
And her jaw
Stretching into a snout.

I dreamed of us waltzing
Across the living room
To the baying of hounds.

I dreamed I rode her horseback
To the Cape Fear Park,
With my hands clinching her mane
While her nostrils flared.

I dreamed of the midnight snack
Of a drunkard
Whose blood made us dizzy.

I dreamed of thirst
And lapping water
Seeing my reflection
I'm a wolf
Like her.

This morning,
My muscles ache.
Dog hair in my mouth.

I told her of my wolfish dreams.
She laughed
And covered her gaping mouth
With blood stained paws.

THE MONSTER MASH

I was sitting in the front seat
Peering through the mist and blades of wipers
Wondering what those things were bouncing
Off the pavement.
At first, I thought it was hail.
Then I realized it was tiny frogs.
Thousands of newborn taking their first
And last leaps into life.
I didn't say anything to my father who was driving.
Sensitive to the vibration of the tires,
Wincing at every thump,
I wondered if frogs had souls
And went to heaven. If they did,
Would they remember the drivers
In the Monster Mash?
This summer before, I had my mom stop
Beside the road so I could get a turtle
Trying to cross.
I was standing five feet away
When a car flattened my hopes to rescue.
That moment I felt amphibiously small, fearful
Of the wheel of death that was set
Into the motion the day I was born.
After a wave of revulsion
And the coppery stench of blood
Was cleansed by the smell of fresh rain
On pavement, I realized how lucky it was
To be alive; that being human meant we had
The facilities to appreciate life,
And not being a mere tortoise
With only the instinct
To seek higher ground when it rained
And to be crushed by something
They never knew what hit them.
I don't like highways or wheels or
Inanimate steel.
The world is one big Monster Mash.

14

A ROSE FOR EMILY

After the eulogy
And everyone left,
A hand dug out of
The grave and snatched
A flower.

BELONGS TO YOU

Miserable
Thump-thump-thumping
Screaming in its chamber
Spitting venom in my veins
Dying
Unless its with you
Thumping in its pain
Broken and calling out
To you
Walking
To your doorstep
Cutting with my knife
Laying it on the porch
Dying
This heart
Belongs
To you...

SHE BRINGS DEAD TIDINGS

She brings dead tidings this writhing sea,
The old man thought
As he watched the coming tide
And the rising tombstone of skeletal light.
He remembered the Manhattan Express of 1938
And felt the tug of his wedding band
As his wife's diamond had caught
As her fingers slipped from his
When the wall of sea came falling
When the wall of death came calling
And swept his wife away.
Does she bring back the dead?
The old man wondered while gazing
Lifting his wedding hand
Into the crested mound of the grave
As he walked into the depths
As he walked into his death
Where his wife lay waiting.

WALKING ALONG A MOONLIT HIGHWAY

I was walking from the lake toward Grandmother's
Along a dark, narrow road, a corridor
Made of cypress trees. I was a child
Again, and the light switch was the other end
Of the highway.
My shadow stretched before me into a lanky praying
Mantis or an alien from War of the Worlds.
Crickets harmonized with my fear, "No monsters here!"
I shouted into the mocking darkness.
And I laughed –
Until an approaching car came from behind
And began to slow.

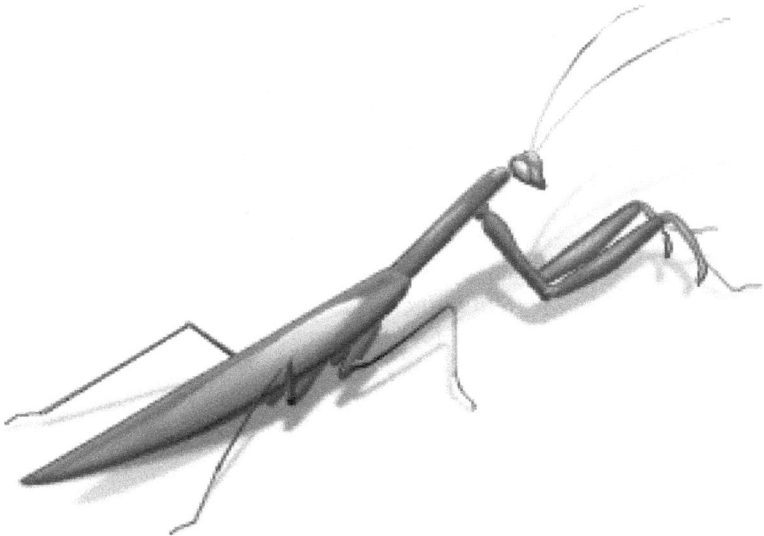

BODY SNATCHER

Flying.
Cold. Falling earthward seeking warmth
To be eaten and
Become nestled in blood and flesh.
This is what I dream about, lying
In the marrow of bones.
Body!
Child looking up for meteorite streaking the sky
To burn his eyes and
Quicken his heart and I will do
All of these things and make him
More than he was and less than he
Is.

Hot!
Ahhhhhh, in the warmth of womb
Red flashing
That blazes my hunger and
Scares me as when in my
Mother's womb a thousand years
Ago
RETREAT!
Talons withdrawn into the pulps
Of thumb pads
So hands can fold in prayer and
Leather wings congeal into the flesh
Of my back and become a throbbing tumor
Waiting…to begin errands of
Destruction.

PHANTOM OF THE CONCERT

Underneath the stands
Of cheering crowds and screaming
Rock and rollers,
Where the popcorn, paper cups,
And roach butts fall, he
Scurries across the floor,
Always in search for a dangling
Foot to pull his victim under.

ROSES AND FANGS

Her lips, a rose upon the snow
When I hissed the soft red
Petal. The tips of my fingers
Froze against her cheek.
I felt the prick of fangs.
Then, slowly the bud opened
With a scent not of roses
But rotting honey bees.
And lying in the grave heart
Was the lustful leech within.

19

THUMP IN THE NIGHT

Thump in the night.
Open eyes.
Something pulls the sheet
Toward the foot of the bed.
Reach for flashlight.
Shine the beam.
Eyes reflect light
And you scream.
Then you realize
It's the cat.

THEY WANT IT BACK

For Halloween, my brother and I
Stole a tombstone from the graveyard.
We hid it under my bed.
The next morning it was gone.
We didn't ask what happened to it.

GRANDMA'S MIDNIGHT SNACK

Grandma's at it again,
Flashing her big brown eyes
With canary feathers
Sticking out of her mouth,
The birdcage still swinging
Back and forth.

Yesterday our cat
Disappeared.

Today, our mail
Didn't come,
And Grandma said
She wasn't hungry
For supper.

I found the mailman's hat
Under the bushes.

Just before bedtime,
I notice Grandma looking at me
Funny with real big eyes.
She reaches for her partials
She keeps in the candy bowl,
And asks if I would like
To be read, "Little Red Riding Hood."

NIGHTMARE ON LIGHT STREET

Rampart heartbeat
Insectile dreams
Rouse me
By the light of the
Orange moon through
My bedroom window
I feel it coming
In the ebb of night.
I watch the narrowing
Of my fingers. Skin
Stretching between
Elongating bones of my arms
And legs to the tip
Of the cartilaginous spur
Of my tail.
There is no flesh between my wings
But only the tissues containing blood
Vessels are nerve fibers.
A claw grows from each hand.
Grotesque leafy membranes
Hang from my nostrils and ears.
My tragus has echoes ringing
Of the insects screaming
Though blind in the dark
With my fur-concealed eyes
I know where they are seeking

The holy lights
Along the streets.
And I am the monster,
The black lightning
Below the Hal-o-scream moon.
I am the vampire of droning
Souls,
The eclipse.
A razor-fanged nightmare's
On Light Street.

BY THE MOON'S GARDENING LIGHT

By the moon's gardening light
Evil sprouts from my skin
Like a dangling cat
From a canine's grin.
Trampling trampling
Paw after paw
Foaming from the mouth
Over teeth and jaw.

By silver and blood
My victim comes,
Stooping and falling
Blood mingled with rum.

Jumping and screaming
I gnaw to the bone,
Slurping and burping
The entrails all gone.

Smacking and clapping
Laughing with glee,
When stomach not growling
I'm human and free.

HAUNTED HOUSE OF HAYMOUNT

I am the edifice of dark emotion.
Listen to the whispers in the vestibule.
Let the stained sheers sway
Your heart
As you descend
Into the foyer for your epiphany
Of horror.
Come see the skeletons
In my closets.
Squeeze the grave dirt
Between your toes in the basement.
Inhale the sweet corruption
Of my rat infested heart.
Stand by the oculus window
And let the moonlight fill your face
With the spirit of ghosts.
Taste the copper memories dripping
From the heat of passions
Of those that died before.
Scream and shake my mortar joints
And become the marrow of my wood.
I am the mausoleum of spirits undying.
I am the phonograph of the dead
With the wind as my needle
Against the eaves.
I play DREAD in FM stereo.
Even with windows bare
No light penetrates my black heart.
If you are evil,
You are home.
And everyone is welcome to my house.

BIRD SNATCHER

Thirteen nights we stayed
In this house by the sea,
Sitting on the porch
Watching storms pass
And never touch us.
We observed the rise and fall
Of a bloated sun and Halloween moon.
We hailed a storm of fallen stars.
Tonight, my heart pangs me
While watching the regular
8 o'clock gull ballet.
I see you standing alone,
Your hands reaching for the birds.

TRANQUIL WACCAMAW LAKE

Life guarding from a cypress knee-root
The yellow wasp surveys
A million bubbles of children
Cascading along the waves.
Nearby a lifeboat is sailing
Its siren quacking alarm;
The tombs of the clamshells are filling
From creatures who come to harm.
Above a helicopter is searching
Along the sunlit crests
For minnows that are surfing
Black submarines are skimming
For crumbles of golden nabs
Amidst the children leaning
For eels, they hope to grab.
By the pier the perch are watching
The ballet of Worm Lake.
The dancers twirl on silver earrings
While puppeteers reel them and wait.
What a suspenseful world it is
Around Waccamaw Lake.
If you find a gleaming pearl, it's
Probably some creature's bait.

UFO RIDE OUT OF HERE

Driving in my muffler-clanging MG with the top down-
Thinking about next week's flight to Kentucky for officer's training-
One eye squinting from cigarette smoke
One hand on the wheel
One hand on the Pepsi
John Fogerty singing "Up and Around the Bend."
I saw it coming from the corner of my eye
This laid down cross drifting in the sky
Except in the middle a bubble – the cockpit
Except where was the sound of the engines
Where was the tail assembly?
I braked to a halt killing the engine
Hearing nothing
Forgetting to breathe
This cross drifting over me
Silent, fifty-feet above the ground.
I opened the door
Take me, I'm ready-
And the ship disappeared over the tree line
Coming as it went
Mysteriously.
I told my mother
She told me to forget about it, keep quiet.

The next day on the news
A UFO was reported.
I called mom at work.
She said it was okay then to tell others.
I wonder if I missed my ride.

WRITER'S WORLD

So the writer types
Inventing another world and characters
Because the world he lives in
Is dull and lonely and stings like a bee

It's safer in the created world
He has control of destinies
And if someone gets brokenhearted
It's because the writer chose it so

In the real life
Important things can fail or leave you
But the writing never goes
It's as faithful as God
As long as the fingers aren't broken
And there's something to scribble on
The creative stories keep coming
Never failing, never really leaving.

CELESTIAL PRIME

We were standing in a winter field
When we spotted Haley's Comet
Making a ghost-like trail across the night.
It was the phantom of the heavens.
It was the omen of our time.
Christina, it was us
In the moment of our prime.

The sight of the milky tail
Shows how simply we exist,
From Apollonius to Caesar, to us when we kissed.
The moment became a travelogue,
A picture in my mind.
Christina, it was us
In the moment of our prime.

And now the nights are empty stages
Years before Haley's monologue.
But if we keep faith with the Starlite theatre
We'll find a comet's mystic fog.
You have to search before you find.
Christina, it was us
In the moment of our prime.

I pulled off the highway and looked across the sky
To find what's now been lost.
I looked to Sagittarius hoping for a sign
Of a fiery sapphire
Blazing a full moon's shine.
Christina, it was us
In the moment of our prime.

RABBIT PAW

After a week of begging
You finally relented and
Took me hunting. You gave
Me your father's shotgun
And showed me the spot
Beside the path
To wait for the rabbit.
You went around the bend
To find another position.

Several hours later
I awakened. Ashamed, I jumped
To my feet and trotted
Down the path.

You were sleeping, too.
Paw prints across your chest.

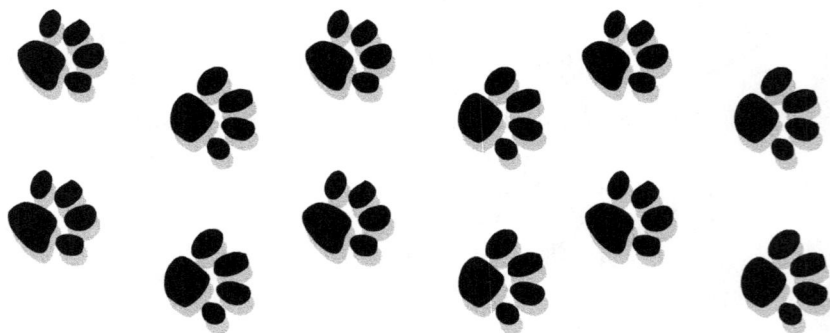

THE FLESH AND SOUL MOTEL

In this heart
Of darkness
Below the marble
Marquee
In this single room,
My soul is boarding
A prisoner in this
Icy chamber
Forever!
Founding, slamming,
Screaming soul,
With the universe
Around me,
I cannot escape,
But lie
In this rotting core
With the worms.
Must I die?
Will I survive,
A soul digested
And squeezed
Through the intestines
Of worms?

Slamming my soul
Against the cardiac muscle,
I discover I can make the cold
Blood pump
Through my desert highways.
Dead
But
Alive,
I claw at the lining
Of my casket
Till the cold
Blood bleeds
From my fingertips
Pounding and pounding,

Dead body, lift these
Frankenstein hands
And tear this heart
From its boney shrine.
Mouth, rip the sutures
From your lips and puncture
This heart with your gold-robbed
Teeth.
FREEEEEEE!
YES!
My soul is free!
Until it crashes
Into the bronze casket.
AGAIN! Again, I was confined.
Must a thousand years
Pass before the rust
Devours the bronze
And sets me free?

Oh, how I cry tears
Of embalming fluid.
The only song to sing
Is the music of
Growing hair and nails.

Oh, how I cry,
With the stars
And worlds waiting
Around me to be ventured.

At night, I hear the moans
Of my brothers. My only
Comfort is knowing, I am
Not alone.

And I wonder
If it was the Devil
Who invented the casket.

METAMORPHOS OF THE WEREWOLF

Ovid you told of the creation
From chaos and wars of discordant atoms
When the universe was lightless
Where heat fought cold
Wet fought dry
Weight contended with weightlessness
Till God settled the argument
Making the eternal order
The force of fire
The celestial heavens
And earth for feet to trod.

From the transformation of
Matter to living bodies
Evil entered the world.
And by the wrath of Jove.
Lycan fled into the silent fields
Escaping the bolt of lightning.
Lycan's screams change to howls.
He tries to talk and spews froth.
His blood thirst rage remains,
Slaughtering sheep
As he trots with body of shaggy hair.
Still Lycan, the bloody eyes,
And bestial savagery.
He transforms his curse
Into a blessing.
Before him the world awaits
Where blood trembles in the veins
Of the sheep.
Lycan howls with moonlit feasts,
And picks the meat from his teeth
With dirty talons. He laps blood,
Not to clean himself, but for the
Taste.
Lycan never dies.
Lycan howls on.

HALEY'S IAGO

Haley's Comet, ghostlike stream
Had drifted while Caesar dreamed.
In Plinty and Lucan's words
A fearful star, burning sword.

This comet that portends doom
Caused our space shuttle to boom
And left us here while we cried
For our astronauts who died.

Haley's Comet, ghostlike stream
Did you bring Aids while we dreamed?
Did you drift over Eden
When the apple was eaten?

The Italians and Russians
Sent satellites for nations
That blinked in Medusa's face
And left their screens black as space.

Haley's Comet, ghostlike stream
Gathers light for children's screams.
Seventy-six years you wait
Never once have you been late.

THE FADE AWAY

How strange to be sitting
On the rocks by the sea
And hear frantic clawing.
I climb down the craggy lair
And find a piece of wood
Wedged between sand and rock.
To my amazement, I discover
Not a plank but a casket is loose
And stands upright.
Any second I except the wood
To splinter by the scratching
From within – a trapped animal?
With all my strength I pull,
And suddenly the casket opens
Leaving me astounded by the
Contradiction of my anxiety.
Her claws soften
Into hands and her smile reminds
Me of a rose upon the snow.
The ringlets of her hair
Concealed her eyes.
She reaches out for me.
When I touch
The lily-white skin
I embrace winter
(Fading)
With a fireplace burning
On my throat.
(Fading)
And I become a tide
Drawn to the dark side.
(Fading)
And I become a tide
Drawn to the dark side.
(Fading)
Where the only sounds
Is a child's laughter
And a screaming soul

Drawn from the warmth
(Fading)
Of its fleshy hearth
Into the dead
Frost of night.
(Fading)
And my body becomes
A shell, whose soul
Is the echo,
Echo of a life now
Faded.

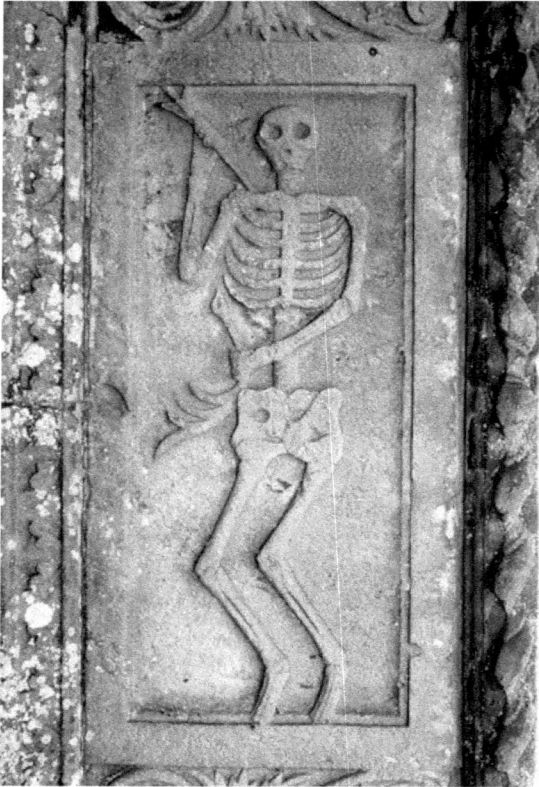

TONIGHT I KILL MY LOVE

Tonight, I will kill my love.
I lay waiting for the sounds
Of her nails as she scales down
The bricks to my window. So silent
Now, I can hear her cold breath
Make mist upon the pane. I feel
Her eyes. Now comes the scratching
Of nails on glass, her yearning
Of entry. For three nights
She has entered and pierced my neck
With fangs. She has sucked blood
From me, talking a part of my soul
With every drop.

The window opens slowly. The sound
Of tongue over teeth clicks
In the darkness. I try to calm
My shaking body. Though my eyes
Are closed. I feel she nears
By the sudden chill and smell
Of unearthed corpses.
I want to scream.
Her hair falls against my chest
Like dirt tossed upon a casket.
I jerk bolt right with pistol aimed
And confront her disarming eyes –
Her Bloody Mary eyes – that make me gasp
And yet willfully bare my throat.

I can feel the cells of my skin
Wanting to flee the wrath of her fangs
As she slowly descends upon my neck.
I want to scream.
I want seduction.
She hesitates with her fangs an inch
From my neck. I can feel the ivory
Cold and the issue of dead breath.
I want the bite of lust.

I want to scream.
Fangs indenting my flesh. Piercing.
Hot blood emptying into the cold black
Heart of winter – into the souls of bats
Flying in the winds of red passion.
I am awakened by screams and morning light.
I am alone, stiff necked, nearly drained
Of blood and soul.
The pistol lies
On the floor.
Tonight, I must kill my love
Before she kills me.

FEAR OF THE LISTENING SOUL

Entrapped in my decaying body,
I can hear the song
Of the woodworms gnaw
Through the casket
In chorus with the rats
Digging through the earth
In search of treasures.

From above, I can hear
The incessant buzz of insects
Upon my drooping roses,
The trod of feet of those
That mourn me,
And the splat of their tears
In the dust.

Anxiously, I pray the trumpets
To sound for the dead to rise.

And I wonder, with the sound
Of gnawing teeth and the squirm
Of worms growing louder,
Can rats eat souls?

ECHOES OF A SEASKULL

How shocked and amazed I was
To find the human skull entangled
In the roots of the dogwood tree.
Such a curious find astounded me.
Carefully, I weighed the skull
In my hands. The cranium was intact
Except for a few teeth missing.
With the precision of a surgeon,
I used a twig and loosened the dirt
That clogged the orbitals.
The suture between the frontal and parietal
Bones reminded me of fragmented china
Glued together.
I suddenly thought of the ocean
With a shore littered with sea skulls.
Thinking this, I lifted the skull
And placed my ear
Against the auditory meatus
And heard the distant echo
Screaming to a sudden horror.
Can skulls capture the sounds of life
Like seashells do the ocean?
Why was there screaming?
I turned the skull in my hands
And found a small unnatural crack
In the back.
A wave of revulsion shook my body.
What happened to this child?
In the throes of death, the
Mother's crying was heard
And retained forever in the skull
Like the rhythmic sounds of the waves
That pound upon the shore.

Vaguely, beneath the scream
The feminine voice sang a familiar lullaby.
I understand, through hearing I see....
The mother walking and singing a lullaby

To the child in her arms.
She trips. The child slips
From her arms and....
I shun the image from my mind.

"Go back to sleep, my little one,"
I whispered into the shell
And covered it with a sheet of sand.

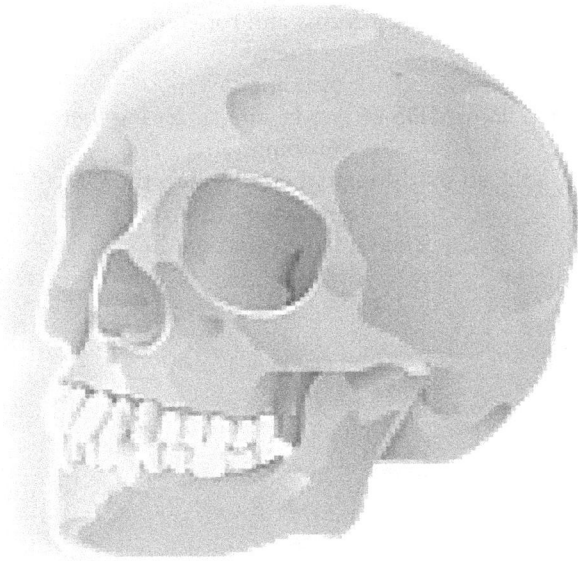

CYCLE OF THE WEREWOLF

Howling....
Werewolf with heroin veins and cyanide eyes
Hunting.....
For virgins to sink his teeth into to squelch his need of
Screaming.....
In his rabid foaming mouth, finding a fix through sex or
Shooting....
Silver drug between his toes, shooting the moon at passing cops and
Cruising....
The bars for young innocents to seduce and bite and make as one and by
Killing....
Them softly with orgasmic dreams and romantic moon songs, he leaves
them
Bleeding...
And crucified with AIDS infested syringes, letting them shriveled and
Writhing....
Needing a fix, so they donate their blood to the Dracula bank for
Spreading....
The virus and starting the

```
                    C
        F                   Y
      L                        C
     O                          L
   W                             E
   E                            O
      R                      E
              E
```

THE DEVIL AND MR. JONES

I touched her
As she lay naked below me.
I burned with lust
Wanting her so-so bad.
The strands of her hair
Running through my fingers.
I smelled her body scent..
In the words of David Bowie
I was, "Putting out the fire
With gasoline."
As I lay upon her
Something uncurled beneath
My body, slithering
And hissing.
I woke from my dream
With the words,
The Devil and Mrs. Jones
The Devil and Mrs. Jones

LITTLE EDEN

Sister Sarah
Walked along the rows
Of strawberries
When she heard the voice,
"Sarah, drink the blood of the Earth."
"What?" she gasped
And felt the bubbling of Earth between her toes.
She fell to her knees before the seeping red.
"Drink, Sarah."
In reverent fear and trembling fingers
She brought the warm liquid to her lips
And tasted
REVULSION – Entrails, the juice of sin.
Turning cold, shivering, spreading from limb to limb
"Sarah, you are now one with the Lord of Darkness,
God of the Earth," the snake hissed from beneath the vine of strawberries.

"Honey? You coming in soon?" called her husband from the porch.
"You know a preacher shan't be late. Service in thirty minutes."
"Your wife comes," she answers. "I think for the next communion, for the
sipping of the wine, we'll have this strawberry juice to be our wine."

KNOCK KNOCK

I dreamed of running down Hay Street being chased by a monster
With the tolling bells of the Market House ringing.
I dreamed about the median of dogwood flowers dripping blood
And their spiny branches trying to detain me.
I dreamed of my bare feet pounding the street as I passed ravens
From Asia cawing for five dollar bills,
I dreamed of the monster's hot breath against the nape of my neck
As I tripped on a crack skinning my knees.
I dreamed the sounds of the galloping claws as the monster
Came trampling to gobble me down and swallow me up,
I dreamed of no pain after my skid of flesh and ran from the monster
Dreamed an idea with no pain in a dream – to break
Into a store and shoot a bullet through my brain,
With marvelous glee for escaping the beast after me,
I dreamed of pulling the trigger with a white blinding flash
Only to find my soul confined in the nightmare
I dreamed that I saw through the eyes of my spirit at the opening
Door and the monster to greet me the one that could defeat me
Was the one they called me.

EGYPTIAN'S DREAM OF AALU

The worm gnawed through my wrappings
While I dreamed of Aalu
Against my eardrum he came rapping
This slithering worm of doom
Praying the Nile to take me
To the land of dread departed
Before the worm devours my dreamed
To join my dead dear-hearted

For written upon my death by law
My beloveth's life be taken
So I would not be alone
In Aalu when I awakened.

Oh Ra! Is it she that sings?
Her voice resounding so clear
Oh Horror! My soul's death screams
It's the worm crawling down my ear.

HEADLINE BLINDED

Because I had volunteered in the emergency room and saw
A grape-faced kid with a razor-blade grin from chin
To chin and he folded his little hand over my thumb,
Because at the Bragg Hotel guys in drag make their money
For heroin sat-AIDS-faction posing with wigs and
Lifting their skirts to show shaven legs and their
Silken crotches,
Because a normal young man crawled through the window to shoot
His mother-in-law, his wife, and son for no apparent reason
Except to slow the scurrying of frantic ants in his
Brain,
Because a drunken driver tried walking the white line with his car
And helped fourteen schoolmates in a bus play hooky for
The rest of their lives,
Because Jimmy Swagged and Jimmy Bakked on TV with their shattered
Crystal churches from believers who threw coins – and down
The house fell and making millionaires from the girls
That dared consecrated seduction to become starlets of the
Centerfield,
Because the young are mining for rose-gold digging with
Their fingers for leftovers for the get rich quick American
Dream with fancy car, psychotic woman with ZZ Top legs
Singing the anthem on MTV,
I've held the patient convulsing with volts frying
His brain while he dreamed in arching yellow streams
And called me Jesus,
Because of sky-sheltered troll children living under the Cape Fear River
bridge, eating rust from aluminum cans that are whitewashed
By passing cars with the wheels splashing dredges of
Humanity of the lushes and lustful into their innocent
Faces covered with festering sores.
Because we are shot, raped, bombed, knifed, molested, murdered, poisoned,
abused, used, neglected, dejected, lied to, threatened, betrayed, and
repeatedly defecated out the bowels of our loved ones,
Because in boring life we seek exhilaration and relief from
Pressure pressure PRESSURES becoming pimp preachers, child beaters,
strip teachers, hostage holders, headline killers.
Because the deprived children of America need attention and will

47

Get it one way or another,
My eyes are headline blinded *because*.....

MY LOVE CAWS

Shut up shut shut up!
Squawk squawk squawk!
You'll drive a man mad, woman!
Shut up shut up shut up.
Can't you let me sleep?
One moment of peace is that too much?
Shut up shut up!
Squawk squawk squawk!
Throwing off the pillow
Rolling over
For a confrontation
SQUAWK!
Long beak! Black eyes!
In a low voice, "Honey, that you?"
SQUAWK!
I scream to flurries of wings
I know I know this is no dream
SQUAWK! SQUAWK!
SHUT UP!
SQUAWK!
I LOST MY MIND!
And to close the deal
She squawks one more time.

NO NO! I want my wife back!
So I plucked one feather at a time
To bring back my sweet wife of mine
I plucked and plucked for an eternal time
And sat in darkness till morning came
When police were pulling me away
From the bed that became her grave
No more squawks but only red
Only silence now that she is dead
I wondered if there is such a thing called Ka
When I heard the raven's caw
As I was am driven away in the back of a car
The raven followed and I knew I'd never get far

RAVEN'S LIGHT

Of black wings spirit bringer of light
Ancient sacred knowledge
Delivered to enlight
Yet known you are
An archetype of fright
Omens of war
Harbingers of death
With your caws and lore
Where death be found
Ravens abound
Eating the flesh of a corpse
Sin eaters without remorse
Yet what is deemed dark in deed
The food the raven feeds
It takes what is dead
Morphing back into living flesh
These things its ingests
From death to life
The Raven's Light

AFTERTHOUGHTS BY AUTHOR

Tale of Waccamaw Lake and BECAUSE were among the first poems I began as a collection of works for SKELETAL SONGS. That was around 1988-89 I think. So tonight, Sept. 30, 2013 I finish the collection for publication finally. What a year it has been. I always knew when I turned 56 years old that either it would be the year I died or something important would happen. Fortunately I deem the latter has happened, though I still have three more months of this year that would be something I had never thought…achieving something important and dying….but that's morbid thinking. I thought 56 was important because my Grandfather Roy Duncan died when he was 56 years old. My Grandfather Fraiser Ward died in 1956.

This year I am marrying my long lost high school sweetheart that has created such a wonderful environment and with her nurse experience and education has aided me to write again, which has always been my heart. In my 56th year, I had my first book published, SWORDSLINGER that went to #1 on Kindle's EBooks in the Contemporary Epic Fantasy genre. Days from now, we are having our second new fantasy saga to be published that is RAVEN'S LIGHT. SKELETAL SONGS will be the third book, but of poetry. In addition, we have begun preproduction of CREMATORY. This is a horror tale that will be published first of 2014. When I finish SKELETAL SONGS today, I will be creating the screenplay for CREMATORY for RAVEN'S LIGHT ENTERTAINMENT whom I have collaborated with its owner of NEW MEDIA. I have to say 56 has been my year of dreams.

Of course each of you who have bought this book and I hope SWORDSLINGER AND RAVEN'S LIGHT, are a major part of the dreams coming true. Thank you my dear readers. I hope my books will continue to rise in popularity and become successful. I am full speed ahead with a dozen books already written and new ones to come. I have always dreamt of being a full time writer. I will always be painting, too. Doing paintings of the stories I write is bringing the two dreams together. Again, thank you! I hope you'll be reading me later. ☺
Stefan Duncan, Oct. 1, 2013

DEDICATION

I like to dedicate this work to my children.

My Step Son Ray Burkle and Joey Boni, who at 10 years old I loved as a son of my own. Ray is getting his English Degree and wants to become a writer. Joey just received his Art Degree and started working in his father's office as an insurance agent specializing with art.

And to my daughter, Abbigail Haven Ward, aka Lady Dragonrose, whose art sings of her own voice.....I felt like Shabael in Raven's Light when he stood by the tower and listened to his daughter's voice sounding like an angel.

And to my step-daughter, Ashley Danielle Purcell, who has given me old cliché' be careful what you wish for, when I always wished of having a big family....by giving me five step-grandchildren (Collin, Reagan, John, Jackson, and Kennedy). I hope one day my grandchildren will think of me as I do my Grandfather Roy, who taught me the Divine lives in nature and of the magic of Lake Waccamaw. Ashley is a constant reader. I encouraged her to start writing. We'll see what will happen with that.

To all of you, my children. Thank you for making feel I have a family.

Love,

Dad/Grandfather

AUTHOR'S NOTE

It's my time to thunder. It is Oct. 2, 2013. The majority of these poems were published in mid 1980's in a little weekend newspaper called the Saturday Extra with the Fayetteville Observer. My intention then was to create a book of poetry that had a combination of scary, dark humored, dance macabre to the music of beautiful, poetic epiphanies.

Before sending to the publisher, I wanted to add several new poems. Usually in the day, I have an idea of what I am going to be writing before I put the hands to the keyboard. I didn't have a chance today though so I just sat down and said, "Let's do it." To my surprise, I ended up doing three with at most 10 minutes in between which astounded me. It was as if I was reliving the 80's all inspired and bursting with things to write.

In the 80's we didn't have e-books and just beginning to have household personal computers. SKELETAL SONGS was supposed to be published around 1990. I remember around 1992 or 3, going to a writer's convention where I first met Lisa Cantrel. During the convention, we were asked if we wanted to read a poem of our own to the several hundred people there. Well, I took my Tale of Waccamaw Lake and read it because it had a good story and had an Edgar Allen Poe ring to it. I remember Fred Chapel was there, a great writer and with the UNC-Greensboro Creative Writing Degree Program. I was asked to read a second poem if I had one. I looked at the sheets I had, then back at the audience and realized out of three hundred or so, 99 percent of them had gray hair and were women. I decided to read, "Grandma is a Vampire." I wasn't sure how it was going to go over, but after reading it with spirit with the last lines about her partial ivory fangs being super glued to her gums…. "So tonight, we'll have to remove her gums." I looked up after that last line and found rows of the ladies laughing with their hands over their mouths. When I saw that I laughed along with them….and, the moment was magical to me. I can't remember what Fred Chapel said word by word afterwards, but I felt truly acknowledged that I was supposed to be a writer. Lisa Cantrel just won BEST NEW HORROR WRITER AWARD for THE DANSE and was secretary of the American Horror Writers Association. She told me the AHWA's Convention to be held several months later in Denver at the Stanley Hotel were Stephen King wrote THE SHINING. I went. While we were on the bus riding up from the airport to the hotel, I had pull out my tape recorder and played the theme song for THE SHINING.

It was an incredible weekend. Two months later, I was at the Warrick Hotel sitting among the greatest horror writers of the world while they voted on horror book contests. I remember being the only unpublished novelist. I was invited to a room where sitting together in the living room were among the six top horror writers of the world. They were discussing the sense of power a guy felt having a remote control, then how one of them had been given the go to do a horror anthology and if anyone wanted to give a short story to it. OMG, I felt I was on the way to breaking into the national level and being right there among the greats.

Unfortunately, my traumatic brain injury got in the way. I was no longer able to read a couple of pages without literally falling asleep. Words scrabbled. I got to a point where I even had to stop being a reporter because I could barely read the story I just wrote to edit it. It was as if the lights were turned off in the room I have always written. I lost my lifelong dream and heart's love to write. I became voiceless. And only years later I discovered that light must have hopped over to my art room. I painted literally from sunup to sundown for 10 years. Then, as you all who know me by now, now I was reunited with my high school sweetheart that is an OR nurse. With her medical knowledge and experience, she recommended a couple of things for me and like a miracle....my writing room light was turned back on.

So tonight, I wrote three poems like the young me prior to my accident. It's been two years or so now that the light's been turned back on. I have a closet full of novels and new ones jumping up and down in my head to start on. I am so exhilarated to be writing again with that burning fire within brighter than I've ever had it. I am back on track now. We will have three books published this year with just as many coming in the years ahead with possible movies.

What got me writing all of this tonight in the author's note is that I went to Barnes and Noble today and bought Stephen King's just released "DOCTOR SLEEP." It was like a sign for me.... It was the return of THE SHINING...to my glory days of writing. King had been involved in an accident also and was knocked off his path in some ways....but seeing "DOCTOR SLEEP" was like a "YEAH, MAN, WE'RE BACK. AND THIS TIME HERE TO STAY."

When it looked for certain that "SWORDSLINGER" was going to be published, I parked my Shadow motorcycle. I was not going to take any chances this time to finally get a published novel out to the world. This week, "RAVEN'S LIGHT" is going to be published with "SKELETAL SONGS" on its wings.

World, hear my thunder! I shout from the mountaintops.....and now eagerly await for echoes. I hope all of you will enjoy my works and pick up on the love I have to write a story. You have bought the ticket. I'm about to give you a ride. I hope I scare you too depths so that when the ride is done, you will have never felt so alive....and maybe...maybe within all the prose, the shocks, the romance, the drama, the laughs here and there....you may find some of life lesson in there like what you get out listening to a Native American tale by a campfire. I love you all and thank you for making my dream as a writer come true.

Your storyteller,
Stefan Duncan, Oct. 3, 2013

One last note: When I sent this off to be published, I felt a tear, then another run down my face. I felt like a little bird that has just flown to ground to snatch up some food and gotten back to the tree without being eaten. I have been underneath it all, terrified something was going to happen before I have a book publish. It all goes back to the first accident and the derailment of my writing career. And now, I have just sent SKELETAL SONGS for publishing. RAVEN'S LIGHT is about to come out in several days. Now that my writing room light is burning, I am working around the clock to get those six novels out I had planned to publish so many years ago and have new ones in between. It is literally a miracle to me to have each published now. It is something I have loved, cherished, dreamt, and died over....to finally come true. I'm going to wipe my eyes now and walk over to Karen and give her a big hug....and you too if I could...

www.ingramcontent.com/pod-product-compliance
Lightning Source LLC
Chambersburg PA
CBHW060722030426
42337CB00017B/2964